VICTORIAN FACTORY LIFE

Trevor May

SHIRE PUBLICATIONS

Published in Great Britain in 2011 by Shire Publications Ltd,
Midland House, West Way, Botley, Oxford OX2 0PH,
United Kingdom.

44-02 23rd Street, Suite 219, Long Island City,
NY 11101, USA.

E-mail: shire@shirebooks.co.uk   www.shirebooks.co.uk

A CIP catalogue record for this book is available from the
British Library.

Shire Library no. 496   .   ISBN-13: 978 0 74780 724 7

Trevor May has asserted his right under the Copyright,
Designs and Patents Act, 1988, to be identified as the
author of this book.

Designed by Myriam Bell Design, France and typeset
in Perpetua and Gill Sans.

Printed in China through Worldprint Ltd.

11 12 13 14 15   10 9 8 7 6 5 4 3 2 1

COVER IMAGE
Shuttle in hand, a weaver engages in conversation with a
young lad in a cramped weaving shed of 1906. We cannot
tell what the working relationship between the two was,
but the number of child workers in textile mills had
greatly declined since the early years of industrialisation.

TITLE PAGE IMAGE
The Derwent Valley in Derbyshire, where a number of the
early cotton mills were located, is an industrial landscape
listed by UNESCO as a World Heritage Site. The early
dependence on water power determined the location of
mills in rural, often isolated areas. The millpond of Richard
Arkwright's Masson Mill is shown here.

CONTENTS PAGE IMAGE
Engineers, millwrights and carpenters (and their dog) at
John Dickinson's Nash Mills, Hertfordshire, c. 1870. Like
any factory, this paper mill could not have been kept going
without such skilled artisans.

ACKNOWLEDGEMENTS
Apsley Paper Trail (from The Endless Web), page 3;
The Bridgeman Art Library, pages 13, 14; Mary Evans
Picture Library, cover and pages 18, 49; Stuart Fourt, title
page; Vik Keshvala, page 20 (top); Lancashire County
Museum Service, with the permission of the Borough of
Blackburn, page 9; Manchester Art Gallery/The
Bridgeman Art Library, page 31; Karin McVicar, page 8;
National Motor Museum, Beaulieu, page 23 (middle and
bottom); National Trust, page 4; Newcastle City Library,
page 36; Oxfordshire Studies, Oxfordshire County
Council, page 23 (top); The People's Museum,
Manchester, pages 32 (left) 44, 47; Ian Petticrew, page 52
(top); Royal Academy of Arts/The Bridgeman Art Library,
page 42; Kara Seaman, page 38; Science Museum,
London/The Bridgeman Art Library, page 35;
A. Walker, page 40; Kotomi Yamamura, page 19 (bottom).

All other illustrations are from the author's collection.

Shire Publications is supporting the Woodland Trust, the UK's leading woodland conservation charity, by funding the dedication of trees.

CONTENTS

INDUSTRIALISATION AND THE FACTORY SYSTEM

B RITAIN accounted for nearly one-third of the world's manufacturing output in 1870. Its nearest rival, the United States, produced less than a quarter. For a generation Britain had been known as 'the Workshop of the World'. We might feel that 'the Factory of the World' would be a more appropriate title, although that description lacks the appeal of alliteration. It would also be inaccurate, for as late as 1901 England and Wales had far more workshops than factories – 143,065 compared with 97,845. Yet the factory remains the dominant symbol of Britain's former manufacturing might, while factory workers are seen as new recruits to the ranks of labour.

In the earliest use of the word, a 'factory' was an establishment for traders engaged on business in a foreign country, the 'factor' being the agent involved in the transactions. The word's modern usage, however, dates from the Industrial Revolution, when specialised buildings came to be used to house new machinery and the army of workers who tended it.

Britain's pre-industrial economy was dependent on agriculture. It has been suggested that around 50 per cent of the population was employed in that sector in 1760, while others were engaged in occupations that were heavily dependent on farming. Many workers serviced the needs of farmers, while a number of industries, such as brewing, soap and tallow making, and the manufacture of leather goods and woollen cloth, relied on agricultural raw materials.

Communications were poor, and most producers catered for a purely local market. Much manufacturing was conducted in the worker's own home, as an adjunct to farming, but the vision of the independent countryman, alternately tending his land and sitting at his loom, is largely mythical. There was no inherent reason why the demands of one occupation should dovetail neatly with the other, for times of frantic activity or sluggishness might easily coincide. The imagined independence of domestic workers is also easy to exaggerate, for they were often tied by debt to the middleman who supplied the raw materials and purchased the finished product. The cottage that is also a workplace can be difficult to live in. Handlooms, though small in

Opposite: Quarry Bank Mill, at Styal in Cheshire, was founded in 1784 by Samuel Greg. Although, by the standards of the time, he was a good employer, the prison-like aspect of the mill buildings would have struck a chord with the early factory workers employed there.

comparison with their mechanical counterparts, took up much space within the home. There was generally no room for power-driven machinery, even if the worker had access to water power.

The capital cost of new power-driven machinery was comparatively low. In 1792 a new forty-spindle spinning jenny could be purchased for £6, while second-hand ones were frequently advertised at a lower price. At a time when domestic hand-spinners might earn two or three shillings a week, the purchase price of a forty-spindle powered jenny was no more than two weeks' wages of the forty female domestic workers it replaced. Factory production therefore paid dividends for the entrepreneur.

Industrialisation brought profound cultural changes to which it could be difficult for the worker to adjust, for factory work led to a loss of individuality and independence. While avoiding the excesses of rural romanticism, it is possible to discern some crucial differences between factory work and that which preceded it. Farm workers might toil from dawn till dusk (or beyond) but work rhythms somehow seemed more 'natural'. However tired or disinclined to work the labourer might feel, it seemed part of the natural order that grain should be harvested before bad weather set in, and that cows should be milked regularly. To be tied to the farm could be harsh, but not as harsh as the slavery of being tied to a machine. In *The Condition of the Working Class in England*, written in 1844–5, but not published in English till 1887, Friedrich Engels, the German socialist and companion of Karl Marx, wrote:

The supervision of machinery, the joining of broken threads, is no activity which claims the operative's thinking powers, yet it is of a sort which prevents him from occupying his mind with other things. We have seen … that this work affords the muscles no opportunity for physical activity. Thus it is, properly speaking, not work, but tedium, the most deadening, wearing process conceivable. The operative is condemned to let his physical and mental powers decay in this utter monotony; it is his mission to be bored every day and all day long from his eighth year. Moreover, he must not take a moment's rest; the engine moves unceasingly; the wheels,

A handloom weaver: woodcut from *The Book of Trades or Library of the Useful Arts*, first published in 1804–5. By 1851, when there were about half a million people manufacturing cotton, there were still fifty thousand handloom weavers.

the straps, the spindles hum and rattle in his ears without a pause, and if he tried to snatch one instant, there is the overlooker at his back with the book of fines. This condemnation to be buried alive in the mill, to give constant attention to the tireless machine, is felt as the keenest torture by the operatives, and its action upon mind and body is in the long run stunting in the highest degree. There is no better means of inducing stupefaction than a period of factory work...

As if to signify that they did not see their employees as rounded human beings, the early factory masters came to refer to their workers as 'hands'. Some went even further. Josiah Wedgwood, the pottery magnate, boasted of 'making such machines of men as cannot err'. Dr James Kay wrote in 1832 that 'The animal machine ... is chained fast to the iron machine, which knows no suffering and no weariness'. The workers were seen as objects – parts of the machines they served. The employers' profits depended partly on the velocity of circulating capital, or the speed with which they could turn over the stock of goods tied up in the production process and in marketing – hence the pressure to keep the machines running. Time was of the essence, and changing attitudes to time were among the most significant changes wrought by industrialisation. For the employer, time was money, to be spent as efficiently as possible. On the other side, workers came to draw a greater distinction than they ever had in agriculture between the master's time and what little they had of their own time, to be used as they pleased. The start of the master's time was often signalled by the factory bell, which the poet William Wordsworth characterised as:

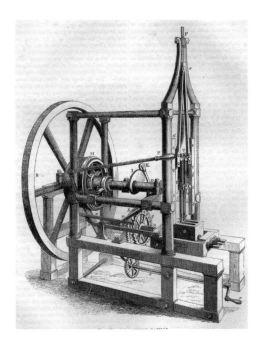

An early example of a mechanised production line consists of the forty-four block-making machines designed by Sir Marc Isambard Brunel for the Admiralty, and installed in Portsmouth Dockyard in the first decade of the nineteenth century, when about 100,000 pulley blocks were required annually by the Royal Navy. Brunel's machines enabled ten men to produce 160,000 blocks a year. The machines remained in use until the 1960s.

Of harsher import than the curfew-knell
That spoke the Norman Conqueror's stern behest –
A local summons to unceasing toil.

Fines were imposed for the slightest lateness, and 'clocking-in' (allegedly introduced by Wedgwood) eventually became standard factory practice. While at their machines, the early factory workers were subjected to other manifestations of 'work discipline'. They could not leave their place for a

'Clocking-in' was a means of enforcing punctuality in factories, and special timing devices were employed for the purpose. This example, manufactured by The National Time Recorder Company, was used at the Verdant Works, Dundee. Clock in one minute late, and you lose fifteen minutes' pay.

drink of water, despite the stuffiness of the workplace, and in many factories they could not use the privy without permission. It was this loss of independent action, rather than the hardness of the work itself, which many operatives resented, and employers felt it necessary to suppress older working habits.

It has been suggested that the work pattern of pre-industrial artisans was not unlike that of today's students — periods of relaxed leisure interspersed with times of frenzied activity as the time for completing a set task approached. In 1842 R. H. Horne reported to the Children's Employment Commissioners on artisan work patterns in Wolverhampton:

> It is as common a thing for a father of a family to be drunk, during the whole of Monday, as for one of the adult workmen who is not married. The women are seldom intoxicated, but give free way to their husbands' love of extravagant and reckless expenditure whenever any money comes into their possession. The family eat and drink it away as fast as they can, and remain in their rags, or domestic want of comfort at home. The majority of the working classes do not work at all on Monday. Half of them do not work much on Tuesday. Wednesday is market-day, and this is an excuse for many to do only half a day's work; and in consequence of attending the market they are often very unfit for work on Thursday morning. Lights are seen in the [work]shops of many of the small masters as late as 10 and 11 o'clock at night, on Thursday. During the whole of Friday the town is silent in all the main streets and thoroughfares, and seems to have been depopulated of all its manufacturers. Lights appear in the workshops to a late hour in the night — sometimes till morning. All Saturday morning the streets present the same comparatively barren and silent appearance. Everybody is working for his life…

The rules of Helmshore Mill, Lancashire, in 1836. Bells governed the worker's day, and 'Any *Weaver* or *Spinner* leaving the Room between Bell Hours, except by leave', was subject to the maximum fine of 1s. 'Quarrelling' attracted a similar fine.

'Saint Monday', as it was known, a holiday for all, was anathema to factory masters, for whom regular working of their machines was essential. Yet it proved hard to eradicate the practice, and absenteeism was rife. Regularity, as well as punctuality, was enforced by fines, and no assessment of workers' wages which ignores this fact is complete.

THE EARLY COTTON MILLS

THE COTTON INDUSTRY came to symbolise the early factory system. Lancashire was its heartland, and Manchester was 'Cottonopolis'. Credit for the first mechanised factory in the world, however, goes to John Lombe, who in 1715 commenced the construction of an austere, five-storey building on the river Derwent at Derby. Lombe imported silk-spinning technology from Piedmont in Italy and may well have been murdered for his pains – an early example of industrial espionage and counter-espionage.

It was cotton rather than silk, however, that pioneered the Industrial Revolution in Britain. The value of cotton exports in 1830 was over forty times greater than it had been in any of the years of the 1780s, and cotton made up 45 per cent of Britain's exports between 1831 and 1850. So much cotton thread came off the machines that Edward Baines claimed in 1835 that the product of one year would stretch from the earth to the sun fifty-one times. By 1851 there were about half a million people manufacturing cotton textiles in Britain, a significant proportion of the almost sixteen million people over the age of nine recorded in the census of that year.

By 1831 the population of Manchester had grown sixfold in sixty years, and by nearly 45 per cent in the previous decade alone. Figures published in 1841 suggested that the life expectancy of mechanics, labourers and their families in Manchester was only seventeen, less than half that of a similar group in rural Rutland, where the figure was thirty-eight years. Manchester had become the 'shock city', at the centre of much social, economic and political debate. The French political writer and historian Alexis de Tocqueville described Manchester as he saw it in 1835:

> A sort of black smoke covers the city. The sun seen through it is a disc without rays. Under this half-daylight 300,000 human beings are ceaselessly at work. A thousand noises disturb this dark, damp labyrinth, but they are not at all the ordinary sounds one hears in great cities. The footsteps of a busy crowd, the crunching wheels of machinery, the shriek of steam from boilers, the regular beat of the looms, the heavy rumble of

Opposite: Pictures are not always easy to interpret. This frequently used image comes from the 1840 novel, *The Life and Adventures of Michael Armstrong, the Factory Boy*. But what does it show? This is only clear within the context of the novel. The two boys at the centre of the image are Michael (on the left) and his crippled brother, Edward. Michael has been removed from the mill and is being raised by the cruel Sir Matthew Dowling, the mill owner. Dowling has arranged this meeting for his cynical self-gratification, and delight at seeing the discomfort of the brothers. Notice the 'piecer,' working at joining broken threads beneath the machine.

Spinning mules at Higher Helmshore Mill, Lancashire.

carts, these are the noises from which you can never escape in the sombre half-light of these streets…

From this foul drain the greatest stream of human industry flows out to fertilise the whole world. From this filthy sewer pure gold flows. Here, humanity attains its most complete development and its most brutish; here civilisation makes its miracles, and civilised man is turned back almost into a savage.

It had not always been thus. The earliest factories had been powered by water rather than by steam, which meant that the best places for their construction, where there was a good head of fast-flowing water, were frequently in rural areas. The remoteness of such places contributed to the difficulty of obtaining a supply of labour, which was one of the reasons why the employment of children proved attractive. The worst features of children's employment were associated with the parish apprenticeship system. Apprenticeship, which was flourishing by the fourteenth century, was a system of training whereby a minor, on payment of a premium, would be bound to a master for a fixed period, during which he would be taught a trade. Alongside this legitimate craft training, a system of parish apprenticeships for children of both sexes was recognised by the Elizabethan poor law. With the assent of two justices of the peace, a poor, illegitimate or orphaned child could be bound to an employer for a fixed term. By the time of the Industrial Revolution, parish apprentices were sent in their hundreds to northern mills, where their role was to attend to the machinery rather than to learn any trade. Effectively, they were sold on by the parish authorities as cheap labour. John Fielden, the factory reformer, pointed out the cynicism of the practice by recounting the case of one parish which contracted to send 'one idiot' for 'every twenty sound children' – a package deal of misery.

The employment of children in cotton mills became an issue of huge controversy in the 1830s and 1840s, with much propaganda both for and against. To Andrew Ure, a Scottish physician who wrote of his visits to English textile mills in 1835, the children resembled 'lively elves' at play. For him:

The doubling room at Dean Mills, Bolton, in 1851, was doubled to make fine thread for the manufacture of lace. Notice the young woman pinning up her hair, which could cause accidents if loose.

Clouds of smoke hang over Manchester. Air pollution was a problem in nineteenth-century factory towns, yet in the popular imagination, ironically, it meant progress, production and profits. A chimney without smoke suggested a stomach without food.

It was delightful to observe the nimbleness with which they pieced the broken ends, as the mule-carriage began to recede from the fixed roller beam, and to see them at leisure, after a few seconds' exercise of their tiny fingers, to amuse themselves in any attitude they chose, till the stretch and winding-on were once more completed.

Was he dreaming, or were his eyes, like those of many middle- and upper-class visitors to the early mills, fixed on the wondrous machines and blind to the workers who operated them? Overseers might have applied threats to make the workers behave well in front of visitors, but the exhaustion of long hours of unrelenting toil must have been difficult to conceal.

On the other side of the controversy there was a sustained and varied stream of propaganda regarding horrific conditions and actual brutality. This encompassed poetry (such as Elizabeth Barrett Browning's 'The Cry of the Children', 1843), novels (such as Frances Trollope's *The Life and Adventures of Michael Armstrong, the Factory Boy*, 1840), and allegedly autobiographical writing, such as *A Memoir of Robert Blincoe, an Orphan Boy* (1832), on which much of Mrs Trollope's novel was based. There were also hundreds, if not thousands, of pages of evidence produced by parliamentary enquiries and commissions, not all of it free from bias. The need to maintain a competitive edge undoubtedly led some employers to extremes, but it would be wrong to condemn a whole generation of factory masters, for there were others who, according to the standards of their time (and the early nineteenth century was an extremely brutal age), acted with humanity.

Supporters of child labour argued that children had mouths to feed, and asked how that was to be done if children did not work. They had a point. The earnings of children were an essential contribution to the family income of the labouring poor. In the early factories there was an imbalance between adult and child labour. For example, at Richard Arkwright's Cromford mills in 1789 there were 150 men in a total workforce of 1,150, or 13 per cent. In the early 1830s between one-third and one-half of the labour force in cotton mills was under twenty-one, and well over half of the adults were women. The man's wage of 10s or 13s a week was less than half what his wife and children might earn from power-loom weaving or worsted spinning. The father's status as breadwinner of the family was undermined, and Richard Oastler, a leader of the factory reform movement, observed that he had witnessed 'full-grown athletic men, whose only labour was to carry their little ones to the mill long before the sun was risen, and bring them home at night long after it had set'. An anonymous report on *Distress in Manchester*, published in 1842, spoke of a family in which the father had been out of work for the previous two months:

> Their only income was the wages of a boy who worked in a factory; these wages, at the present high price of provisions, would not supply the boy alone with sufficient food; his mother said that he more frequently returned to his work without tasting food than with a tolerable meal. Her husband had at first, when his own work entirely failed, refused to taste the food purchased with his son's wages, which he insisted should be reserved for him; but since his intellect had become deranged he seized and devoured with greediness whatever food came within his reach.

Clogs were the typical footwear of textile workers well into the twentieth century, and they were to be found in many other occupations. Their perceived association with poverty, and a growing use of steel toe-capped safety boots, led to their gradual decline from the 1920s.

Cutting the Straw

Sorting the Straw

Making the Straw Plait

Joining the Plait

Sewing the Plait into hats by Machine

Sewing the Plait into hats by hand

Pressing hats by Machine
Crimping a Dolly Varden

Pressing hats by hand

STRAW-PLAIT AND BONNET-MAKING AT LUTON.

THE RANGE OF FACTORY WORK

IT WOULD be a mistake to think of the worker in a cotton mill as the typical factory worker, or even that there was such a person as 'the typical cotton worker'. In 1841 the census recognised over a thousand subdivisions of heads of employment in cotton manufacture alone. Throughout the nineteenth century the principal division was between skilled and unskilled workers. Even this apparently simple distinction has its complexities, for 'skill' is to a large extent a subjective concept. All occupations would like to consider themselves skilled, as it is often the path to higher pay and social status. The key issue is to agree upon the particular characteristics that denote skill. Throughout history it has often been men who made that judgement, and naturally made it in their own interest. The historian Maxine Berg has observed that 'the knacks, the deftness and the special application' with which women worked in many trades were regarded not as 'skill' but as 'female characteristics', to be rewarded accordingly – or not rewarded at all. Furthermore, the comfort of the factory worker and his family was heavily dependent on the ability of the woman of the house (whether employed or not) to manage a budget, to cook and to make or repair clothes, all done without any direct payment. Even today, a distinction is made between women who go out to work and those employed in unpaid 'housework'.

Apart from overseers or 'gaffers', mule-spinners were the highest-paid operatives in the cotton mill. While average pay levels in the mills were low, the rates of male workers were high (though there were not many of them). Figures from one small spinning mill of the 1830s show that forty workers were employed, but half of the weekly wage bill was paid to just four mule-spinners.

The skilled and the unskilled maintained their separateness outside the factory as well as within it. In the late 1890s Allen Clarke, a native of Bolton, wrote:

> No spinner with any self-respect in his stomach would drink beer in the tap room with a common labourer; he must have his ale clad in shining glass, not paltry pot, and enjoy it in the company of his own class, or at least with

Opposite: Bonnet-making at Luton: engraving from the *Illustrated London News*, 7 December 1878. The quality of local wheat straw made Luton a centre of the straw-hat industry from at least the seventeenth century. Domestic workers in Bedfordshire and Hertfordshire produced the plait in strips, and this was made up into hats in Luton factories and workshops.

engineers and other artisans of the elevated grade, who had the time o'day and night told to them by gold watches with conspicuous chains to match. Among the blue-blooded and wealthy upper circles, there could not be any sterner divisions of caste than those separating one section of working-folk from another at this time.

Factory women exhibited similar characteristics. In Glasgow before the First World War (and probably elsewhere) there were separate clubs for 'hat girls' and their inferior sisters, the 'shawl girls'.

The early textile factories were water-powered and in general were quite small. Their often remote location required entrepreneurs not only to draw in labour, but to provide the necessary infrastructure. This included housing, as well as the means to provide their workers with the basic necessities of life – hence the introduction of the company-owned 'tommy shop', where goods were sold at inflated prices to the millhands. The introduction of steam power made a significant difference to industrial location, and it became possible to establish factories, of much greater size, in the towns. However, the change did not come overnight. As late as 1839, when there were 3,051 steam engines in the textile factories of the United Kingdom, there were still 2,230 waterwheels.

Not all factory workers were employed at machines, for there was a need for some clerical workers. Their working conditions were usually superior to those of the factory 'hands'. This office is in the restored Higher Helmshore Mill.

Robert Owen sought to create an ideal working community at New Lanark, near Glasgow. This was one of the most publicised social experiments of the nineteenth century and in the ten years from 1815 attracted nearly twenty thousand visitors. This print of 1825 shows girls at his school dancing the quadrille.

Manchester came to symbolise the industrial town, but it did not provide a unique model. There were other kinds of industrial town, which followed a different pattern. Prominent among these were Birmingham and Sheffield, the former a centre for the manufacture of small metal items, the latter for the manufacture of cutlery. The typical form of industrial organisation in these towns was the small workshop. Small masters (or 'little mesters', as they were known in Sheffield) were self-employed craftsmen, either working alone or taking on a small number of assistants, and who rented (and sometimes owned) workshops, where they concentrated on a single aspect of the total production process, such as shaping, grinding or finishing. Employer and employee worked closely together, and the worker might reasonably hope, one day, to set himself up in business. Birmingham and Sheffield have therefore been described as cities of social cohesion, for employer and worker had similar interests. On the other hand, Manchester, where most workers stood little chance of acquiring the capital to establish a factory, and where millowner and mill-worker rarely saw each other, has been seen as a city of social conflict.

STAMPING THE PEN FROM THE STEEL.

In some instances, what appeared to be a 'factory' could more accurately be regarded as an agglomeration of workshops. This was true, for example, in the great Soho Foundry at Smethwick, which Matthew Boulton and James Watt had established for the manufacture of steam engines. In reality it was an amalgam of workshops in which skilled craftsmen were employed on piecework. By the Factory and Workshop Act of 1878, a general distinction was drawn between factories and workshops, the former being defined as places where machinery was

Above right: Cutting the blanks of pen nibs from a steel strip: an engraving from *The Boy's Book of Industrial Information*, 1863. The requirement to stand, and the repeated swinging of a heavy bar, could be very tiring, yet concentration had to be maintained in order to avoid accidents with the unguarded punch.

Right: In the 1860s about one hundred firms were engaged in the Birmingham pen trade, although it was dominated by about a dozen. In 1819 James Perry, a schoolmaster, began making steel pens by hand, having found existing ones unsatisfactory. Perry's pens were originally made in Manchester, and then London. From 1829 they were made by a Birmingham manufacturer, but the name continued until 1961.

used, worked by steam, water or other mechanical power, while in the latter it was not. But there was a list of nineteen classes of works which were defined to be factories and not workshops, whether mechanical power was used in them or not. 'Factory work', therefore, included work in a variety of mills, works, workshops, shipyards and steam-powered laundries.

Production organised through interlocking workshops was particularly efficient in those industries where the product was dependent on fashion and great flexibility was necessary in order to keep up with changes in the market. London, the centre of fashion, had many such industries, including the furniture industry. Whole streets in Hackney, in the East End of London, were organised like a production line, but with a series of small workshops engaged in just one part of the production process. So diverse were London's industries that it is easy to forget that, in terms of total production, London was the principal industrial city of Victorian England. Land values, which were very high there, militated against sprawling factories, although London did have some very large works. Mechanical

Above left: Cradley Heath, in the West Midlands, was a centre of the chain-making industry. The work was undertaken in small workshops, where masters and their employees were paid by the piece. The conditions in such workshops were as bad, if not worse, than any to be found in a factory. This workshop, which lacks the clutter and dirt of the original, was re-erected at the Avoncroft Museum of Historic Buildings.

Left: Suspended like scenery at a theatre, huge lengths of floor cloth dry in the Knightsbridge factory of Smith & Baber. As London did not have a single dominant industry like Manchester or Sheffield, its industrial strength in Victorian times is often ignored, but it probably had a wider range of factory-based industry than any other place in the country.

engineering was for long concentrated in the capital, where it was pioneered by the redoubtable Henry Maudslay. Through his workshops passed hundreds of engineers, a number of whom went on to great renown, including James Nasmyth, inventor of the steam hammer, and Joseph Whitworth, the standardiser of screw threads. Maudslay had

Right: At the end of the nineteenth century there was much concern over 'sweated labour'. Employers reduced their overheads by employing outworkers on piece rates. Competition between workers desperate for employment kept wages low. This page from *Punch* in 1888, when many Jewish refugees from Russia were moving into the East End of London, a centre of the tailoring trade, has strongly anti-semitic overtones.

Below: Workers at the Royal Arsenal at Woolwich, London, coiling bars for the manufacture of the Armstrong gun in 1862. Many factories depended on military contracts, for supplying products ranging from uniform buttons to huge naval guns.

started out as a workman at the Woolwich Arsenal, a vast industrial complex in south-east London which, at its peak, during the First World War, extended over some 1,300 acres and employed around eighty thousand people.

Manchester, Leeds, Clydeside and Tyneside, as well as London, became centres for the manufacture of machine tools and other kinds of engineering. Agricultural engineering, on the other hand, was located in country towns. For example, Ransomes had a factory in Ipswich, Garretts were based in Leiston, Suffolk, Burrells were to be found in Thetford, Norfolk, and Ruston & Hornsby had their home in Lincoln.

It is easy to imagine a north and south divide in regard to factory production, but many factories were located in small country towns. Witney in Oxfordshire had a blanket factory, which was renowned for the quality of its products. Luton was a centre of the straw-hat industry, which depended on domestic straw-plaiters and factory-based hat manufacturers. The villages around Kettering, Wellingborough and Northampton were full of outworkers making shoes. Attempts to introduce machinery and factory methods into the shoe industry were evident from the middle years of the nineteenth century, but it was not until the mid-1890s that, outside of the high-class bespoke trade, the factory triumphed.

Looking like something from the set of Charlie Chaplin's film *Modern Times*, this was the largest crane at the Woolwich Arsenal at the end of the nineteenth century. Much heavy lifting in Victorian factories was done with human muscle power, but not the 110-ton naval gun shown here.

Whipping the edges of blankets in a factory in Witney, Oxfordshire. Witney was an ancient wool town, which became pre-eminent in the manufacture of blankets. The last mill closed in 2002.

Assembling cars at the Coventry Motor Company in 1897. Only hand tools are in evidence. Coventry changed its industrial base over the course of time. Originally a centre of silk manufacture, by the late nineteenth century it was associated more with the manufacture of bicycles and motor cars.

Ford opened a factory at Trafford Park, Manchester, in 1911. By 1914 the company had installed an assembly line for the manufacture of the Model T, the wheels for which can be seen being gravity-fed to the assembly line below. The assembly line led to a loss of job satisfaction, which placed a strain on labour relations.

HEALTH AND SAFETY

PARTICULAR GROUPS of workers have always been exposed to industrial
hazards. However, the advent of mechanised factories led to fresh
dangers, while new processes in such industries as the manufacture of
chemicals, and the use of those chemicals across a range of industries,
contributed to an increase in industrial disease. Factory legislation gradually
came to tackle these problems, but in an age of *laissez-faire*, when decision-
making was determined largely by market forces, there were always those
who saw regulation as leading to a loss of competitive edge. Many
manufacturers exhibited an almost cavalier regard to sickness and accident.
Leonard Horner, one of the first factory inspectors appointed under the
Factory Act of 1833, observed in his report for 1845 that:

> When I view the complicated machinery amongst which people work, the
> infinite number of wheels and other mechanisms, with projections to catch,
> sharp edges to cut, and vast weights to crush, the crowded state in which the
> machines are often packed together, and the great velocity and force with
> which they move, it often appears to me to be a marvel that accidents are not
> a daily occurrence in every mill.

It was all too easy for clothing to become entangled in machinery, or snatched
by the belts which transmitted the power to it, but there was a widespread
reluctance on the part of early factory masters to incur the expense of fencing
shafts and gearing. Employers in industries other than textiles could be
equally casual. In 1842 R. H. Horne reported on Hemingsley's nail and tip
manufactory in Wolverhampton:

> Not any of [the] machinery is boxed off, or guarded in any way … It is a
> frightful place, turn which way you will. There is a constant hammering roar
> of wheels, so that you could not possibly hear any warning voice …You have
> but once to stumble on your passage from one place to another, or to be
> thinking of something else, and you are certain to be punished with the loss of

Opposite: Casting
a massive cylinder
for the frigate
HMS *Agincourt*
at Maudslay &
Company's
foundry, London,
in 1862. Burns,
both minor and
serious, were not
uncommon, and
the health of
foundrymen was
further damaged
by the alternation
of searing heat and
sometimes biting
cold as they toiled
in sheds that were
often open-sided.

Fire was an inherent danger in factories. The Factory and Workshop Act of 1891 laid down that new factories employing forty or more persons should have a fire safety certificate. This fire alarm is one of a number installed in the early twentieth century at the Royal Gunpowder Mills, Waltham Abbey, Essex, where the consequences of a fire would be especially serious.

a limb, or of your life if the limb does not come away kindly … Little boys and girls are here seen at work at the tip-punching machines (all acting by steam power) with their fingers in constant danger of being punched off once in every second, while at the same time they have their heads between two whirling wheels a few inches distant from each ear … 'They seldom lose the hand,' said one of the proprietors to me, in explanation; 'it only takes off a finger at the first or second joint. Sheer carelessness – looking about them – entirely through carelessness!' … At this manufactory fingers are pinched off at the tip-turning machine; punched off at the punch-engines; and smashed (perhaps the whole hand) by the tip-hammer.

Horne observed that for the carelessness of one second a child might be mutilated for the remainder of his or her life. The casualties of the factories were to be encountered on the streets of industrial towns. Engels wrote of Manchester in 1844:

Besides the deformed persons a great number of maimed ones may be seen going about Manchester; this one has lost an arm or part of one, this one a foot, the third half a leg: it is like living in the midst of an army returning from a campaign.

Of the Welsh iron-making town of Merthyr Tydfil, the local surgeon claimed that there were 'more men with wooden legs than there are to be found in any town in the kingdom having four times its population'.

Many features of the factory environment might exacerbate the problems of accident or poor health. Bad flooring might be a hazard. R. H. Horne wrote of Hemingsley's factory (mentioned above) that:

The flooring was so broken that in many places I could look down into the room below through the gaping and rotten planks… I mentioned its unsafe condition, but my apprehensions were smiled at as groundless, and treated lightly. A few days afterwards a part of the upper floor fell.

The danger of tripping up near dangerous machinery might be increased by poor lighting. Marshall's Temple Mill, a flax-spinning mill at Holbeck, near Leeds, overcame the problem of poor light in that it was a single-storey structure (unusual in the 1840s, when it was erected), with ample top-lighting. This was provided by more than sixty glazed cupolas, some 14 feet in diameter, looking like 'cucumber frames in a garden'.

Textile mills stank from the animal fat used as a lubricant, and the urine used in the fulling process. Temperatures were kept artificially high. Allen Clarke wrote of cotton mills in 1899 that:

> The humid atmosphere promotes perspiration, but makes evaporation from the skin more difficult, and as a result the underclothing becomes moistened. In this condition the operative, when he leaves the mill, and has to face a much-reduced temperature, is most liable to take cold, which may be the forerunner of some serious chest affection.

Extremes of temperature were perhaps worse for foundry workers, who were often employed in open sheds, with the hellish heat of the furnace in front of them and biting winds at their back.

Individual industries had their particular diseases and ailments. One of the worst affected was the textile industry, which had a workforce of over a million by 1891. In carding rooms in particular, where the cotton fibres were straightened, the air was thick with fluff and dust. Bessy, a character in Mrs Gaskell's novel *North and South* (1854–5), described the 'luff' (fluff):

> ... little bits, as fly off fro' the cotton when they're carding it, and fill the air till it looks like fine white dust. They say it winds round the lungs, and tightens them up. Anyhow, there's many a one as works in a carding-room, that falls into a waste, coughing and spitting blood ...

A variety of bronchial and respiratory complaints ensued, including byssinosis, or 'brown lung disease', which is peculiar to cotton workers.

Overhead shafts and belts at Masson Mill, Cromford, Derbyshire. Innocuous-looking while at rest, they could maim and kill when in motion. Despite this, there was much initial opposition to fencing them in.

A file-maker at his bench. Warrington was the main centre for this trade, which could cause serious deformities to the wrist and hand of the worker.

Girls packing matches in a London factory. Although 'safety matches', made from harmless red phosphorus, had been patented in 1855, the public preferred the white phosphorus variety, even though it caused a necrosis of the jaw among women workers handling it. The use of white phosphorus was made illegal in 1910.

Male mule-spinners, who were once estimated to walk 20 to 30 miles a day as they tended their machines, were prone to contract cancer of the groin from the continual contact with the oiled moving parts of the mule. When weaving sheds were introduced, cancer of the mouth could be caused by 'kissing the shuttle' as a means of drawing through the thread. Children, whose bones were growing, were likely to develop weak ankle and knee joints, which often seemed to seize up on Monday mornings, after a day of rest.

It was possible to guess at the industry in which a worker was employed from the physical symptoms of industrial disease that were displayed. Potters suffered from 'potter's rot', a form of asthma (resulting from the ingestion of fine dust from calcined bones, flint and clay) that was peculiar to them. The phthisis, or tuberculosis, that dry-grinders in the Sheffield cutlery industry suffered from was similarly called 'grinder's rot'. Repetitive strain injury affected workers in many industries. including file-making:

Making felt hats at
a hat factory:
an engraving from
George Dodd,
*Days at the
Factories*, 1843.
Mercury was used
for the curing
of pelts, and the
noxious fumes
that are given
off can lead to
neurological
damage. This
provides
circumstantial
evidence for
the origin of the
phrase 'as mad as a
hatter', but this
explanation is not
accepted by all.

> The right hand … has frequently a marked distortion. Almost everything it
> holds takes the position of the file. If the poor man carries a limp lettuce or
> a limper mackerel from Wolverhampton market, they are never dangled,
> but always held like the file. If he carry nothing, his right hand is in just the
> same position.

Match-makers, who until late in the nineteenth century were obliged to work
with white phosphorus, succumbed to 'phossy jaw', a painful necrosis, one
of the more bizarre symptoms of which was that, in the dark, affected bone
would glow with a greenish tinge. Felt-hat makers and those who used
mercury to silver mirrors suffered from loosened teeth as well as cramps
and tremors, while lead poisoning was the lot of workers in a wide range of
factory occupations, including printing, paper-colouring, and the
manufacture of linoleum and floor coverings. Those who produced white
lead suffered the most. One of the effects was 'wrist drop'. Robert
Harborough Sherard met a sufferer in the 1890s:

> He could only lift his arms with the hands hanging down, and to raise a glass
> to his mouth had to press it between the backs of his wrists. He has to eat
> like an animal, with his mouth to his plate. He is completely helpless at the
> age of thirty-nine… 'I shall never be able to work again,' he said.

As factory legislation expanded in scope, the issue of industrial health was
tackled both on a general basis and in relation to particular industries.

Above: A safety notice at Masson Mill, Cromford. Pressure of work frequently obliged workers to ignore such legal prohibitions.

Above right: Packing bleach in the chemical works of Widnes or St Helens.

Just as not all millowners had supported the fencing of machinery, so not all workers welcomed the control of dangerous industries. Some workers involved in factory processes that were particularly harmful to health felt that their wages incorporated an element of 'danger money' and feared that their pay would go down if the risks were significantly reduced. The statistics of death from toxic trades probably underestimate the problem. As R. H. Sherard wrote of the chemical industry:

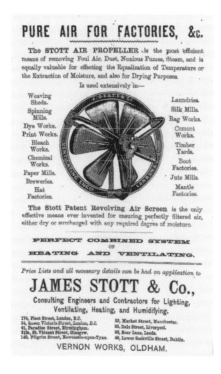

[If] the published statistics show but a small death-rate in the chemical trade, it is because the chemical yard only kills a man three parts out of four, leaving the workhouse to do the rest.

The future must often have looked bleak to factory workers, but at least the ironworkers of Merthyr Tydfil had something to

Left: The Factory and Workshop Act of 1878 empowered factory inspectors to order mechanical ventilation to be installed where dust was generated and inhaled by workers to a dangerous extent.

look forward to. As the *Merthyr Guardian* announced in July 1843:

> COFFINS – It is not perhaps generally known that the iron masters supply their workmen with wood to make their coffins. [Quoted by Keith Strange]

Limited redress was offered by Parliament. The Employers' Liability Act of 1880 placed the onus on workers to sue their employer, and the burden of proof lay on them. They were not protected from injury caused by a fellow worker. This Act, amended in 1897, was replaced by the Workmen's Compensation Act of 1906, a piece of legislation which had teeth, but was full of complexities. L. G. Chiozza Money MP, who was one of the drafters of the Bill, admitted: 'The law … is necessarily complicated, and I, who helped to make the law, always take care to look it up before I dare define liability under it.'

Slain by 'Roger'. 'Roger' was the name given by alkali workers to clouds of chlorine gas, which, pumped on to slaked lime, transformed it into bleaching powder. It was observed that 'Roger … is so poisonous that the men … work with goggles on their eyes and twenty thicknesses of flannel over their mouths … A "feed" of this gas kills its man in an hour.'

Above: Eyre Crow first exhibited his painting *Dinner Hour, Wigan* in 1874. Crowe has clearly romanticised the scene, in which refined-looking millgirls have their hair in smart snoods to keep it away from the machinery. Food often had to be gulped down in the shortest possible time, and it was not until the end of the century that widespread provision was made for eating meals.

WOMEN IN THE FACTORIES

THE TOTAL NUMBER employed in factories in the United Kingdom in 1896 was 1,184,431. A total of 528,795 were employed in cotton mills, of whom 320,000 were women. Throughout the nineteenth century the textile industry was the largest employer of industrial female labour, although women employed in domestic service far outnumbered the rest. While factory owners valued women as a source of cheap labour, many middle-class people were troubled at the impact of factory employment on the supply of suitable servant girls. In 1842 R. H. Horne, a sub-commissioner of the Children's Employment Commission, wrote:

> A girl who has been accustomed for years to a workshop or manufactory, or a pit-bank, can scarcely ever make any of her own clothes, cook a dinner of

Right:
A 1908 poster for the Artists' Suffrage League by Emily Ford. Towards the end of the nineteenth century there was a fierce controversy over the issue of protective legislation for women. Some feminists were infuriated by the idea that women were weak and could not fend for themselves, arguing that restrictive legislation prevented women from competing with men in the labour market.

the plainest description, or reckon up a weekly bill. She would be a treasure, indeed, that could … Few people will receive [former factory girls] as house-servants – partly on account of the associations to which they have been subject in the shops and manufactories; partly because their habits render them anxious to have their evenings 'out' – and partly because they really understand no sort of household labour.

The anxieties of the servant-keeping class were also directed at the impact of factory employment on morals, with much concern expressed at the alleged licentiousness in workplaces that employed both men and women. Much of this concern was ill-founded, although it could be difficult to maintain standards of common decency in factories where toilet facilities were inadequate or non-existent.

It would be a mistake to assume that women necessarily disliked factory work, especially as the century progressed and working conditions improved. There is evidence that some young women valued their independence so highly that they delayed marriage in order to enjoy a regular wage and the fellowship of their co-workers. Older women, too, might welcome a return to the workplace after the loneliness of the home. Allen Clarke said that he

Opposite page, bottom right: A Cradley Heath chainmaker making dog chains, 1897. Workers, many of whom were women, were paid by the piece. The work, carried out in small workshops, could be heavy, and wages were low. Sold for 1s 6d in the shops, each chain she made earned her ¾ d. Working ten hours a day, she could make six chains, which brought her in the princely sum of 4½ d.

Left: With rare exceptions, early factories did not provide childcare facilities, but a number of employers took up the idea later in the nineteenth century. This nursery was provided by Pretty & Son at their corset factory in Ipswich. The attention of trained nurses, together with two meals a day, was provided for 2d. Other employers refused to employ married women.

had 'often heard married females say that they would rather be in the factory than in the house, because the comparative isolation gave them the dumps after being used to the company of hundreds of workmates'.

In the early stages of industrialisation it was frequently necessary for women to work, for without their contribution (and that of their children) the family could not survive. Women might work to within a day or two of the birth of a first child and would often get back to work within a week of confinement. Not until 1891 did the Factory Act prohibit the employment of women within four weeks of confinement. Dealing with babies and toddlers (often a task for baby-minders) was difficult, and recourse was frequently made to 'quieteners'. Popular throughout the century was Godfrey's Cordial, a generic name for a concoction containing opium that pharmacists made up themselves. R. H. Horne interviewed a pharmacist in Wolverhampton in the early 1840s:

> There is a quack or patent medicine called *Godfrey's Cordial*, of which great quantities are sold in Wolverhampton. It is a mixture of boiled treacle and water, with the addition of a certain portion of opium… Many children are killed by it. Some waste away to skeletons, and their sufferings are prolonged; others die more easily. Every chemist and druggist here makes his own *Godfrey*. It is left to the apprentice to concoct, or to the chemist's wife. It stands in a great jug on the counter for sale. They are all obliged to keep this medicine, or they would lose their custom. Not one of them

Music while you work, 1905. Women pack Erasmic soap and scent at the Warrington factory of Joseph Crosfield & Sons. The firm had 'trained the girls in certain departments to sing part songs, which they are encouraged to do at certain hours while they work'. No doubt this practice also discouraged them from singing their own songs, which, by all accounts, could be very bawdy.

probably could reply to the question of what quantity of opium there was in a quart of his *Godfrey*. He does not know. He does not know, because his apprentice or his wife made it…

The hours and conditions of women, children and young persons became increasingly regulated from the 1840s, when they became classed as 'protected persons'. Belief in the freedom of contract, and the idea that male workers were free agents, made it impossible for reformers to tackle men's hours head on. But it was conceded that women and children needed 'protection', and the regulation of their conditions became a Trojan horse which reformers thought would force employers to make concessions to all workers. Women working in textile mills were limited to ten hours a day in 1848, and so interconnected were the processes in which men and women were involved that it was thought that this would soon herald the ten-hour day for all. But the Act did not limit the amount of time that the engines might run, and through a system of shift working employers were able to resist change.

Munitions workers at the Kilnhurst Steel Works, Rotherham, making artillery shells in 1918: a painting by Stanhope Forbes. It is easy to exaggerate the long-term impact of the First World War on women's factory employment. Heavy work was not new and was common in a number of industries.

THE FACTORY
WORKER AT HOME
AND AT PLAY

WHEN STEAM POWER brought factories into the towns, there was an immediate housing problem, of a kind familiar in the developing world today. To give but one example, the population of Bradford grew by 65.5 per cent between 1821 and 1831. By 1841 the city had a population of 34,560; in 1851 it had risen to 103,778. Not only were there more people to house, but there was a great demand for land from industrialists, and for building up the infrastructure. Railways scythed great swathes through the towns, adding to the general pressure on the accommodation of workers.

There were several ways that the demand for living space could be met. Existing houses could be subdivided to squeeze more people in. In the 1860s Liverpool's population density was 66,000 per square mile, giving each resident little more than 5.5 square metres of space. Existing cellars could be used, and new ones created. Manchester had eighteen thousand cellar dwellings in 1843, housing around 12 per cent of the population. John Adshead wrote of the town in 1842 that:

Murton Working
Men's Club sword
dancers in 1904.
Murton, near
North Shields
on Tyneside, was
largely a mining
village. Sword
dancing has a long
history and shares
its rural origins
with a number
of leisure activities
pursued by factory
workers, including
pigeon-fancying,
the keeping of
whippets and
greyhounds,
and gardening.

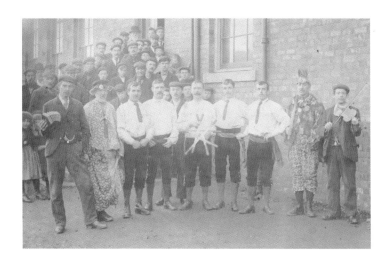

it must be borne in mind that the cellars which are used as habitations by the poor have no other feature in common with the cellars attached to the middle class of dwelling-houses than that of their being below the level of the street. They are most of them neither drained nor soughed. They are consequently damp, – are always liable to be flooded, – and are almost entirely without the means of ventilation…

A cheap way to build mass housing was in the form of the back-to-back, where terraces of houses shared a common back wall, standing one on each side of it. Apart from those at the end of a terrace, this meant that three walls were shared, with the only light and air entering from the front. Yet such houses were not unpopular with workers, for what the houses lacked in light and air they made up for in warmth. In the mid-1880s over 70 per cent of the houses in Leeds were back-to-backs, and they continued to be built there until 1937, despite a by-law prohibition imposed by the city in 1866, and a general prohibition set out in the 1909 Housing and Town Planning Act. As with so many things in Victorian Britain, there was often a huge difference between passing a law and enforcing it.

Rent was a significant part of the household budget for the Victorian factory worker, and the range of housing reflected this. Widows often took in lodgers in order to get by, although those living in company housing might face eviction. How much comfort workers found at home depended on many things.

A tin bath in front of the fire was the lot of most factory workers (if they were lucky). This late-nineteenth-century house at Bourneville had a bath let into the kitchen floor, hidden by a trap door when not in use.

A lithograph of houses erected at Preston, Lancashire, from an 1844 report. It was noted that 'Each back yard is furnished with a privy by the landlord, and, in many cases, with a pigsty and its attendant midden by the tenant… It is right to state that the inhabitants of the cottages do not complain of annoyance from these reservoirs of filth.'

Back-to-back
houses in Leeds,
still going strong
in 2010.

Many homes were comfortless, sometimes because incomes were low, sometimes because domestic skills were lacking. The poor often struggled valiantly to make ends meet, to feed themselves and their children, and to keep themselves clean, against all the odds.

It is difficult to pin down wages, although it is safe to say that for much of the time many workers found it hard to make ends meet. Across the whole range of factory work there was considerable variation in money wages, depending on the degree of skill of the worker and fluctuations in trade. Periods of unemployment would bring down the average. It has been shown, for example, that a Leeds weaver who nominally earned 13s a week had an average wage of only 10s 10d when two months of unemployment are taken into account, while a dyer, whose nominal wage was 22s (when employed), had an average weekly wage of only 16s 10d when three months of unemployment are taken into account. Similarly, at times when there was a heavy demand for manufactures, and order books were full, bonuses might be paid – either in cash or in kind, through the provision of food or drink. Some workers were paid by the piece rather than by shift, which further complicates the picture, while others enjoyed perquisites (or 'perks') such as the right, increasingly disputed by employers, to take scrap materials. Finally, we need to think in terms of family income, rather than that of a single breadwinner. In the textile industry, for example, the earnings of a wife and two children might double the wages of the husband.

Historians have written extensively about whether the standard of living of the mass of workers rose or not during the Industrial Revolution. The unrest of the early part of the nineteenth century might suggest that it did not, but it is equally possible that the discontent was directed more at the quality of life, for, as has been pointed out, the transition to factory work and its attendant discipline proved irksome to many. From the 1850s, however, the trend is much clearer. For the majority, things were getting better.

In a study of late-nineteenth-century Liverpool dock workers, the social reformer Eleanor Rathbone (great-granddaughter of Samuel Greg of Quarry Bank Mill) observed that times of food shortage were not compensated for by times of plenty. She noted:

> In the matter of food even less than the other necessaries of life, an irregular supply is not the equivalent of its average since neither physiologically nor in any other way can privation at one time be compensated by a surfeit at another.

In Frances Trollope's novel *The Life and Adventures of Michael Armstrong, the Factory Boy*, Mary Brotherton, a sympathetic character and the daughter of a millowner, was of the opinion that 'a great deal of good might be by teaching them [the factory workers] a little economy, and inducing them to lay by their superfluous money in a savings bank'. She had the grace to admit, however, that she knew little about the reality of their lives. There were many members of the middle class who were equally generous in offering advice, and equally ignorant. If the workers could have eaten the cookery books written for them they would never have gone hungry. Recipes for economical meals abounded. They included such delights as stewed ox cheek and mutton chitterlings – or small intestines. The latter were to be obtained immediately after the animal had been killed, scoured many times with salt and water, and soaked for twenty-four hours. All this would make them white and free from smell. They possibly tasted good, too. But the writers of such recipes completely ignored the fact that working women lacked both the time and the inclination to cook any food that required such lengthy preparation. They wanted their food hot – and they wanted it quickly. If at all possible, they also wanted it unadulterated.

R. H. Horne wrote that in Wolverhampton in 1842:

> Great quantities of bad meat are sold in the market, particularly veal. The worst description of this bad meat is not brought into the market till after dark, and is chiefly furnished by the

The shop in Toad Lane, Rochdale, established by the Rochdale Equitable Pioneers Society, an early venture in co-operative shopkeeping, which opposed the adulteration of food and the selling of inferior provisions to working people. While not the first example of co-operation in shopkeeping, the Rochdale Pioneers set the pattern which the later co-operative movement was to follow.

An advertisement for Gainsborough Working Men's Club, Lincolnshire. (Notice the use of an older spelling of the place-name.) The club was established in 1870 'To afford the Industrial Classes the means of social intercourse, mutual helpfulness, mutual and moral improvement, and for affording facilities for holding meetings of Friendly and other Societies'.

country butchers, who have it ready for the 'fitting hour' in their carts just outside the town. The stalls are lighted up with candles so as to throw a strong light upon the best joints, or those that can be made to look best, while all the remainder is in the shade. I am of opinion that the lean of the stale meat is tinted up with fresh blood, and the fat parts powdered with some white composition. I am led to this opinion from the fact, that, while my eye was attracted by the brightness of the red and white, my nose was repelled by the same object.

When associated with the truck system, food adulteration was particularly heinous. Workers were obliged to purchase provisions from the company 'tommy shop', already mentioned, where what they bought (often above the market price) was set against their wages. Anything that could be adulterated generally was. The addition of sand and dirt to sugar added to its weight. With similar intent, flour was mixed with alum, chalk or pipe clay. Milk was watered down before being thickened again with chalk and flour.

Especially in the early days, the daily round of the factory hand was hard – sleep, work, eat, sleep. Little wonder that so many workers were exhausted, or that they sought solace in drink – the quickest road out of Manchester. There was little time for recreation. As late as the 1890s, Allen Clarke wrote:

The factory operatives do not read much, and study little. As I have said before, their day's labour unfits them for any real mental work. They seek light amusement when their toil is done. They patronise the football matches in thousands. They want no lectures on science, ethics, culture; they have no desire for art galleries; they are so ignorant of Nature that they have little love for rural strolls; all they crave is stirring excitement or full rest from their labours. And can we blame them?

One can sense here the disappointment for his class of the self-educated man. Clarke was born in 1863 and worked in the mills from the age of eleven.

He became a successful writer of poetry and novels, as well as antiquarian, philosophical and political works. Not all were like him, but he seems to ignore the fact that the range of leisure activities of factory workers, as of other members of the working class, was immense.

For some, leisure hours were taken up with the competitive growing of fruit or vegetables (the first national register of gooseberry competitions was published in Manchester in 1786). For others it was racing pigeons (the first meeting of the National Homing Union was held in Manchester in 1897). Some played football or supported a local team, which sometimes originated in a factory or works team (Arsenal was formed in 1886, as a works team from the Woolwich Arsenal). Music was the enthusiasm of others, with brass bands and choral singing particularly popular (Halifax Choral Society, founded in 1817, claims to be the oldest amateur choir in Britain having a continuous performance history). And some just wanted to sit at home and put their feet up. As Allen Clarke said, 'can we blame them?'

Mill girls in the northwest of England developed their own clog dances, based on the 'click' and 'clack' sounds of the textile machinery. The popularity of North West Women's Morris has now spread far beyond the region where it originated.

Above: This 1872 engraving by Gustave Doré vividly captures the spirit of the 'penny gaff', a rowdy precursor of the music hall, popular with factory workers and other members of the working class. The social reformer James Hole, a committee member of the Leeds Mechanics' Institute, in 1860 complained that one such gaff 'has a larger nightly attendance than the evening classes of all [Leeds's] seventeen Mechanics' Institutes put together'.

OUT OF WORK

THE DAILY TOIL of the factory worker was often hard. Even harder was life without work. Workers might find themselves unemployed for many reasons. Accidental injury and industrial disease have already been discussed. A study of unemployment published in 1911 spoke of a former Birmingham factory worker:

> He has lost all his lower teeth through lead poisoning in the factory where he used to make medals, etc.; he suffers from colic and is turned 60; it is fourteen years since he had any regular work; he is now fit for nothing but carrying sandwich boards and doing odd jobs.

It was in 1911 that unemployment insurance was brought in by Part II of the National Insurance Act. The scheme at first covered only a limited number of trades, whose members were ordinarily well paid (and could therefore afford the contributions) but who were liable to severe unemployment at times of trade depression. These included building, shipbuilding, mechanical engineering, ironfounding, vehicle construction and saw-milling. Employees and employers each paid a third of the cost, with the government paying the rest. The years 1912 to 1914 were generally prosperous, and so the scheme was not immediately put to the test, but the limited strain which the scheme could bear was revealed in the dark days of unemployment after the First World War.

Changes in demand for a factory's products could be seasonal or brought about by the workings of the trade cycle, with its attendant booms and slumps. An example of seasonal variation is afforded by the history of Wall's. Thomas Wall was a well-established London butcher by the beginning of the nineteenth century, and built up the family business in selling meat and meat products, receiving several royal warrants. However, trade fell off sharply in the summer months, leading to the laying off of staff from their factories in Battersea and Acton. An alternative product was needed to even out production and retain staff, and in the early twentieth century it was decided to diversify into ice cream. The First World War started before the plans could be implemented,

Opposite: Hubert von Herkomer's painting *On Strike* was first exhibited at the Royal Academy in 1891. With his back to the wall, the striker reveals the tension of his situation in the way he twists his cap. He is clearly torn between a duty to support his workmates and the duty to support his family, whose suffering is expressed in his wife's face.

A brass doorplate from one of the early labour exchanges, the first eighty-three of which were opened in 1910. At first some employers opposed them, fearing that they would be a refuge for the work-shy. At the same time some workers feared them as possible places for the recruitment of blacklegs during labour disputes.

Opposite: A soup kitchen set up in Manchester by the Society of Friends (Quakers) in 1862 to relieve workers made unemployed by the disruption in supplies of cotton during the American Civil War.

and it was not until 1922 that the first Wall's ice cream went on sale.

Even a booming industry might experience seasonal unemployment. The cycle industry is an example, with demand for bicycles highest in the summer. It was recorded in 1896 that a Coventry company employing seven hundred in the summer expected to dismiss 'the large part' over the winter. Asked what happened to them, a company representative replied: 'If they belong to a union, like the blacksmiths, they apply for out of work relief, and others shift for themselves.'

In some industries it might be possible to cushion the blow, and to retain skilled labour, by stockpiling, but only to a limited degree, and not without reducing rates of pay. Iron puddlers in Merthyr Tydfil were earning up to 50s a week in the good times of 1838; by 1840 this had fallen to 20s, and by 1849 it was 19s or less – a fall of over 60 per cent in little over a decade. In the 1850s and 1860s, after fresh deposits of ironstone had been discovered in the Cleveland Hills, the iron industry of north-east England overtook that of south Wales, and many Welsh ironworkers migrated to Middlesbrough. Others emigrated to the United States, helping to build up the industry of that country.

They were not the only workers who sought to escape the threat of unemployment and to seek better conditions in America. The Cobden Treaty in 1860 removed trade barriers between Britain and France. Within a decade, the importation of cheap French silk helped send the British silk industry into a continuous decline. In 1851 nearly 131,000 had been employed. By 1907 this had fallen to just over 32,000. Hundreds of Macclesfield silk workers emigrated to Paterson, New Jersey (whose own silk industry had been started by a Macclesfield man), with the result that it was said that people in Macclesfield, in regular receipt of letters from relatives and friends in the United States, spoke of Paterson as though it were just down the road.

During the American Civil War (1861–5) Manchester was gripped by the so-called 'Cotton Famine'. Like many historical events, however, the story is not as simple as it first appears. Union forces blockaded Confederate ports, preventing supplies of cotton from getting through. However, it now seems clear that the Lancashire industry would have experienced a depression even without the Civil War, for there had been gross overproduction in the 1850s, accompanied by much speculation. There was much cotton stacked away in Lancashire warehouses, the owners banking on higher prices as the war went on, and even re-exporting it to American factories through such ports as New York. By October 1861 Manchester mills were closing for lack of raw material, and by November of the following year 331,000 men and

PREPARING THE SOUP.

THE MAZE

THE DISTRIBUTION

women were idle – three-fifths of the cotton operatives were out of work. The respectable suffered along with the improvident. Soup kitchens were opened, and much charitable aid was received. Many workers, however, felt that charity had not begun at home, that much of the aid had come from outside the area (which was true), and that the cotton masters had taken their responsibility to their workers lightly. Unrest was inevitable, and there were riots in 1863. Not until April 1865, when the Civil War ended, did things begin to return to normal.

The Cotton Famine highlights the strained relations that often existed between employer and employee. This was especially apparent in those industries where there was little prospect of the worker becoming his own master. There were two possible responses that the worker might make. One was to attempt to overthrow the capitalist system and to replace it with socialism. The other was to accept capitalism, but to join with others to gain greater security and a better position within the system. At different times in the nineteenth century each of these approaches was tried. The Amalgamated

A cartoon from *Punch*, 17 January 1852, on 'The Effects of a Strike'. In fact, the outcome of industrial action depended on a number of factors, especially the labour scarcity of the workers involved, and also the state of trade.

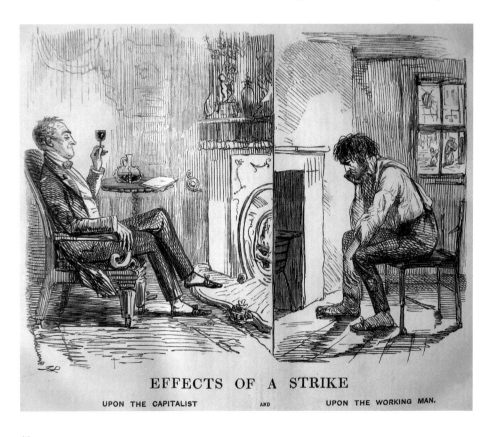

EFFECTS OF A STRIKE

UPON THE CAPITALIST   AND   UPON THE WORKING MAN.

Society of Engineers, which catered for many of the most skilled men working in factories, was formed in 1851 and was the first of what came to be called the 'new model unions'. With a membership of better-paid workers, such unions could charge a higher rate of contribution of around 1s a week. This enabled the unions to provide a wide range of benefits, covering unemployment, sickness and superannuation. They also assisted members to emigrate, viewing this as a means of maintaining the scarcity value of their members at home. As these benefit funds grew, union leaders sought to protect them by avoiding strikes wherever possible. 'Never surrender the right to strike,' said Robert Applegarth, general secretary of the Amalgamated Society of Carpenters, 'but be careful how you use a double-edged weapon.'

The banner of the Manchester District of the Amalgamated Society of Engineers, Machinists, Millwrights, Smiths and Pattern Makers. The ASE, established in 1851, represented skilled craftsmen of the so-called 'aristocracy of labour'. Factories could not have been run without them.

Unskilled workers, including many of those to be found in factories, lacked the greater security of those with a trade skill. However, by the end of the nineteenth century the distinction between the skilled and the unskilled became less clearly defined. This was particularly noticeable in the engineering industry, where the introduction of automatic and semi-automatic machinery led to a growing class of 'semi-skilled' workers. Even labourers came to have a 'special value' to many employers, who began to appreciate that modern factory methods required, above all, a stable labour force.

In 1888 a strike that eventually brought out seven hundred match girls in London gained a significance out of all proportion to its original small scale. The cause of these women, many of whom suffered from a most debilitating industrial disease, was taken up by middle-class reformers (including George Bernard Shaw, who was treasurer of their strike fund). The success of the two-week strike was followed by a strike of London gas workers, early in 1889, and later in the year by the great London Dock Strike.

Although members of the so-called 'aristocracy of labour' might bewail their loss of status, the events of the late nineteenth century may have encouraged many to throw in their lot with the working class as a whole, which has led some historians to argue that it was only then, rather than much earlier, that a true working-class consciousness came into being.

FACTORY LIFE AT THE END OF THE VICTORIAN PERIOD

ALTHOUGH to many workers the monotony of the daily grind must have seemed unremitting, the late-Victorian factory was in many respects very different from its counterpart at the beginning of the reign. No longer was it possible to describe Britain as *the* workshop of the world. By 1913 Britain had fallen to third place in manufacturing, with only 14.1 per cent, behind the United States and Germany, with 35.3 and 15.9 per cent respectively.

Some sectors of industry continued to hold their own, such as the older branches of the engineering industry, including railway locomotives and textile machinery. Platts of Oldham, for example, employed twelve thousand workers in 1914 and produced as much textile machinery as the entire American industry. Britain was heavily dependent on a narrow range of staple industries. The Census of Production of 1907 revealed that coal, textiles, iron and steel, and engineering accounted for about 50 per cent of net industrial output and employed one-quarter of the occupied population. In contrast, only just over 5 per cent of industrial employment was in the newer industries such as electrical goods, road vehicles and man-made textiles such as rayon.

While these broad trends are indisputable, a factory worker of the 1830s, transported to a factory of the 1890s, would have noticed many differences. Children were still present, but in far smaller numbers. Education was now perceived to be the proper occupation of childhood, and children were seen as an investment for the future rather than an essential part of the labour force. Safety in the workplace was now taken more seriously, and the number of factory inspectors had risen from a handful in the 1830s to around two hundred by the end of the century, including women (the first two female inspectors being appointed in 1893).

We should beware, however, of seeing the story of Victorian factory life as one of continuous and inevitable progress. The desire of Josiah Wedgwood, the pottery magnate, to make 'such machines of men as cannot err' was shared by many industrialists at the end of the century, when 'scientific management' became a new watchword. Imported from the United States, this business strategy is associated with Frederick Winslow Taylor, who at the turn of the century was management consultant to the Bethlehem Steel Company, described at the time as 'the world's most modern company'. Together with others, Taylor introduced time-and-motion studies in the 1880s, and he brought all his ideas together in 1911 in his book *The Principles of Scientific Management*. Taylor advocated getting rid of rule-of-thumb methods, the simplification of the worker's tasks, and the identification and use of 'the one best method'. He was contemptuous of 'craft pride' and advocated practices that would maximise the employer's profits but also offer higher wages to the worker. The process was one of 'de-skilling' and had the unfortunate effect of removing much satisfaction from the employee. Workers came to take an 'instrumental' view of their work – something to be endured to earn a wage. For the unskilled, this had perhaps always been the case, but for those with a hard-earned skill the change was one to be resisted.

As employers sought a stable workforce, there was a fresh espousal of the idea of the factory as a community, and a number of British companies experimented with company villages, offering their workers (and sometimes

Dancing on the pier at Blackpool, c. 1897. The practice of mills in individual northern towns shutting down for 'wakes weeks' gained ground at the end of the century, enabling groups of work companions and their families to holiday together. In 1883 773,213 excursionists visited Blackpool. Special train fares were made available, and lodgings were cheap.

The girls' dining room at Cadbury's factory, c. 1905. A 'roast and 2 veg' cost 4d, a meat pie 2d, or soup and bread 1d. Alternatively, food brought in from home could be heated up.

others) improved housing. This was often accompanied by a range of welfare benefits, either free or at a subsidised rate. These included medical aid, dining services, and social and recreational facilities. In some ways this represented 'welfare capitalism', whereby the employer met many of the worker's needs, but at the price of banning trade-union activity within the works. In 1905 Budgett Meakin wrote, in mechanistic terms, of the advantage to an employer of providing recreational facilities for workers:

In the 1890s attempts to introduce automatic and semi-automatic machinery into engineering workshops met stiff resistance from skilled engineers and fitters, who feared their work being taken over by unskilled men. A strike led to an employers' lockout, running from July 1897 to January 1898, by which time 47,500 men had been locked out by over seven hundred firms. This *Punch* cartoon shows a fitter berating a union official. 'You've nearly brought us to that,' he exclaims, as he points to the workhouse.

[It] is only where high spirits and enthusiasm enter the human machine that, like a well-oiled engine, all the parts work smoothly and produce the greatest effect with the least friction.

The pioneer of the later nineteenth-century factory villages was Sir Titus Salt, a Bradford wool merchant and manufacturer, who specialised in the alpaca market and had developed mixed fabrics that combined alpaca and mohair with cotton and silk. By 1850 he was operating five mills in Bradford, and in that year he decided to move them all outside the city. A site was found 3 miles from Bradford, on the river Aire (hence the name – Saltaire). When opened in 1853, it was the largest mill of its kind in the world. The village followed the building of the factory, and by 1871 it contained 4,300 inhabitants in 824 houses. None of the houses was back-to-back, and all were larger than the customary workmen's cottages of the time. Furthermore, they were all connected to a main sewage system. For Salt, the venture was a mixture of sound business sense (he looked after the health and stability of his workforce) and Christian charity. He took a paternalistic interest in his village. While cleanliness might be next to godliness, it was not to be advertised by unsightly washing hanging on lines. He provided amenities for the recreation of the residents, but this did not extend to the provision of a public house. Salt died in 1876, and by the end of the century Saltaire appeared rather dowdy in comparison with other planned villages.

J. & J. Colman, mustard manufacturers of Norwich, had by the early twentieth century a number of staff dining rooms spread across various departments, with meals costing from 2d to 4d a dish. This illustration shows the glass case by the factory gate, 'wherein are displayed each day, as in a "cook-shop" window, priced specimens of the viands to be obtained'.

Port Sunlight, begun in 1888, and now containing nine hundred Grade II listed buildings.

Cadbury's Bournville Works provided cycle sheds for their workers, with compressed air laid on to inflate tyres. The smart outfits of these young women suggest that they were company clerical 'staff' rather than factory 'hands'.

Port Sunlight was an altogether leafier place, with cottages in an 'Olde English' style, in stark contrast with most workers' housing. Its founder, W. H. Lever (later Lord Leverhulme), a grocer by trade, became engrossed with the possibility of mass markets in household necessities. He was a marketing man rather than a technologist and came up with popular brands such as Lux, Vim and Sunlight soap. Originally these were made for him by an outside supplier, but in 1885 he bought his own soap works in Warrington. Dissatisfied with the cramped site, in 1887 Lever purchased 52 acres (later extended to 500 acres) on the Cheshire side of the river Mersey, near Birkenhead. Here he built a soap factory, together with a village to house his workers. The women workers started ten minutes after the men and left the factory half an hour earlier. In a passage titled 'Raising the Tone', Budgett Meakin observed that:

> Where large numbers of girls and men are employed it has been found worth while arranging for them to come and go separately, thus avoiding an unseemly rush for train or tram, or any opportunity for horse-play.

Cadbury's kept men and women apart as far as possible, admitting only 'red badge men' (who, like prison 'trusties', wore a red armband) into the women's departments. The company insisted that women wore white holland overalls (blue in the case of forewomen), the material for which was, in the first instance, provided free, and afterwards at a subsidised rate. Ten years before Port Sunlight commenced manufacturing, Cadbury's moved their works to Bournville, on the outskirts of Birmingham, where they created 'the factory in a garden'.

Bournville differed from some factory villages in that the houses were not confined to employees. By 1905 only about two-fifths of the tenants worked for Cadbury's, and about an equal number commuted into Birmingham for other employment. Because rentals had to be kept within the means of residents, the houses were more modest than in places where a philanthropic employer was prepared to subsidise his workers. Houses on the 458-acre site varied in style and size to meet the requirements and means of occupants. All the

George Cadbury, the confectioner, relocated his factory from Birmingham to rural surroundings at Bournville, 4 miles away. From 1893 to 1900 Cadbury acquired around 300 acres of land, upon which he laid out a model community. This illustration, c. 1900, shows a group of cottages with rentals of 7s 6d and 8s 3d a week.

houses contained a bath – located in a bathroom in the better houses, or hidden beneath a lid set into the kitchen floor of the most basic properties.

In York, another Quaker chocolate manufacturer, Joseph Rowntree, shared a sense of responsibility for his employees. He established sick and provident funds, and provided the services of a doctor to his workers without charge. A dentist similarly treated employees, although 6d was charged for gas, 'if desired'. In 1901 Rowntree purchased 150 acres at New Earswick as the site of a workers' village. It was laid out by Raymond Unwin and Barry Parker, for whom this was their first important planning commission. Unwin and Parker went on to pioneer town planning and improved housing, using their experiences of factory communities to inspire a national movement for better housing.

A greater interest in scientific management at the end of the nineteenth century led larger employers to set up personnel departments. Rowntree, the chocolate manufacturer, appointed the first woman 'social secretary' in 1891, to look after the interests of female employees. The original caption to this picture read: 'One of Messrs Rowntree's social secretaries engaging a new "hand".'

FURTHER READING

Bailey, Peter. *Leisure and Class in Victorian England*. Methuen, 1987.

Bell, Lady Florence. *At the Works. A Study of a Manufacturing Town*. Thomas Nelson, 1911; reprinted, Virago, 1985.

Benson, John. *The Working Class in Britain 1850–1939*. IB Tauris, 1989.

Burnett, John. *Plenty and Want*. Routledge, 1989.

Burnett, John (editor). *Useful Toil. Autobiographies of Working People from the 1820s to the 1920s*. Allen Lane, 1974.

Burton, Anthony. *Remains of a Revolution*. Penguin, 2001.

Chapman, Stanley D. (editor). *The History of Working-Class Housing*. David & Charles, 1971.

Clarke, Allen. *The Effects of the Factory System*. Grant Richards, 1899; reprinted, Nabu Press, 2010.

Clayre, Alasdair. *Work and Play: Ideas and Experience of Work and Leisure*. Weidenfeld & Nicolson, 1974.

Crooks, Eddie. *The Factory Inspectors*. Tempus, 2005.

Darley, Gillian. *Factory*. Reaktion Books, 2003.

Dodd, George. *Days at the Factories*. Charles Knight, 1843; reprinted, Augustus M. Kelley, 1967.

Engels, Friedrich. *The Condition of the Working Class in England*. 1845; new edition, with introduction by Tristram Hunt, Penguin, 2009.

Ereira, Alan. *The People's England*. Routledge & Kegan Paul, 1981.

Flint, Kate. *The Victorian Novelist: Social Problems and Social Change*. Croom Helm, 1987.

Freedgood, Elaine. *Factory Production in Nineteenth-Century Britain*. Oxford University Press, 2003.

Gauldie, Enid. *Cruel Habitations: History of Working Class Housing, 1780–1918*. Allen & Unwin, 1974.

Jennings, Humphrey. *Pandaemonium. The Coming of the Machine as Seen by Contemporary Observers*. Andre Deutsch, 1985.

Lavalette, Michael (editor). *A Thing of the Past? Child Labour in Britain in the Nineteenth and Twentieth Centuries*. Liverpool University Press, 1999.

Meacham, Standish. *A Life Apart: The English Working Class 1890–1914*. Thames & Hudson, 1977.

Meakin, Budget. *Model Factories and Villages*. T. Fisher Unwin, 1905; reprinted, Kessinger Publications, 2009.

Owen, Robert, and Claeys, Gregory (editor). *A New View of Society*. Penguin Classics, 2007.

Sherard, Robert H. *The White Slaves of England*. James Bowden, 1897; reprinted Nabu Press, 2010.

Shill, Ray. *Workshop of the World: Birmingham's Industrial Legacy*. Dutton, 2006.

Simmons, James (editor). *Factory Lives: Four Nineteenth Century Working-Class Autobiographies.* Broadview, 2007.

Strange, Keith. *Merthyr Tydfil, Iron Metropolis: Life in a Welsh Industrial Town.* Tempus, 2000.

Thompson, E. P. *The Making of the English Working Class.* Penguin, new edition, 2002.

Trollope, Frances. *The Life and Adventures of Michael Armstrong, the Factory Boy.* 1840; reprinted Nonsuch, 2007.

Vincent, David. *Bread, Freedom and Knowledge: A Study of Nineteenth-Century Working Class Autobiography.* Methuen, 1982.

Williams, Alfred. *Life in a Railway Factory.* Sutton, 1992.

Wohl, Anthony. *Endangered Lives: Public Health in Victorian Britain.* Methuen, 1984.

PLACES TO VISIT

The decline in Britain's manufacturing sector has been accompanied by a proliferation of heritage sites commemorating the industrial past. Many factories have been opened as museums, some with working machinery. Others have been preserved but put to new uses, ranging from luxury apartments to craft workshops and retail outlets. Five (out of around thirty) of UNESCO's World Heritage Sites in the United Kingdom relate to industry. These are: Blaenavon Industrial Landscape, the Derwent Valley Mills, Ironbridge Gorge, New Lanark, and Saltaire.

A number of gazetteers include factories and related buildings open to the public. Two which can be recommended are:

Burton, Anthony. *The Daily Telegraph Guide to Britain's Working Past.* Aurum Press, 2002.

Dibnah, Fred, and Hall, David. *Fred Dibnah's Industrial Age.* BBC, 1999.

The National Trust is custodian of a number of sites, including Quarry Bank Mill at Styal, Cheshire, and back-to-back houses in Birmingham. In every case it is sensible to visit websites in order to check current opening times.

INDEX